Harry Eagleson
Pasadena, 1932

NICODEMUS

BY EDWIN ARLINGTON ROBINSON

COLLECTED POEMS
  AVON'S HARVEST
  CAPTAIN CRAIG
  CAVENDER'S HOUSE
  THE CHILDREN OF THE NIGHT
  DIONYSUS IN DOUBT
  LANCELOT
  MERLIN
  TRISTRAM
  THE MAN AGAINST THE SKY
  THE MAN WHO DIED TWICE
  THE THREE TAVERNS
  THE TOWN DOWN THE RIVER

CAVENDER'S HOUSE

ROMAN BARTHOLOW

SONNETS 1889–1927

THE GLORY OF THE NIGHTINGALES

THE THREE TAVERNS

TRISTRAM

MATTHIAS AT THE DOOR

NICODEMUS

A BOOK OF POEMS

By Edwin Arlington Robinson

NEW YORK

The Macmillan Company

1932

PRINTED IN THE UNITED STATES OF AMERICA
NORWOOD PRESS LINOTYPE, INC.
NORWOOD, MASS., U.S.A.

TO
EDWIN CARTY RANCK

Nicodemus, Toussaint L'Ouverture, and *Ponce de Leon* appeared first in the Yale Review; *Annandale Again, Hector Kane,* and *The Spirit Speaking* in Scribner's Magazine; and *Sisera* in The Theatre Arts Monthly. The author's thanks are due for permission to include these poems in this volume.

CONTENTS

NICODEMUS

If held and questioned amiably, no doubt
Caiaphas would have said he was a priest,
And not a prophet; and he might have said
That his eyes rested well on what they saw,
And that his ears required no crash or murmur
Of innovation for their daily music.
There were some rumors, but he smiled at them
And all who heeded them, and shook his head
Reprovingly, as at uneasy children;
And so he smiled tonight at Nicodemus,
Who had come late. More like a fugitive
He looked, in a long cloak that covered him
With dark humility that composed itself
Conveniently with night, than like a lord
At home in his own city; and Caiaphas,
Greeting him, asked him why.

                "Why do you wear
Your shroud while you are living, Nicodemus?
And a black shroud at that. Why do you pay
For noble robes and cover them with a sack?
Are you afraid of robbers?"

"No—not robbers."
And sighing as he said it, Nicodemus
Sat gazing at a darkness on the floor,
Where the black cloth had fallen. "No—not
   robbers."

"You are afraid of something, Nicodemus.
I have had fear myself, and know the signs.
I was afraid once of an elephant.
There are no elephants in Jerusalem.
What is it then that ails you? If I know,
There is no need of asking; for your coming
Like this would be an answer. Was he pleased
With your accommodation of your graces
To the plain level of his lowliness?
I have been told he was a carpenter—
Before he was a . . ."

        "You may go as far
As that, and frequently," said Nicodemus,
"And find yourself as far from the same word
As you are now. He was a carpenter;
But there are men who were dead yesterday,
And are alive today, who do not care
Profoundly about that. What the man is,
Not what he was to unawakened eyes,
Engages those who have acknowledged him
And are alive today. Though he has wrought
With common tools, he does not ask of us
That we be carpenters."

[2]

Caiaphas laughed unheard,
And curled a quiet lip. "I am glad of that;
For you might cut your finger, Nicodemus.
And what's all this that you are telling me
Of men dead yesterday and still alive?
I do not know such men, and would far rather
Not meet them in the dark."

"It is not there
That you are like to know them, Caiaphas.
They have come out of darkness—where we are,
I fear, and where I fear we may remain.
High men, like you and me, whether by worth,
Or birth, or other worldly circumstance,
Have risen to shining heights, and there may still
Rise higher, where they shall be no higher than
        earth.
Men who are braver may forgo their shining,
Leaving it all above them, and go down
To lowliness and peace, and there find life.
Caiaphas, you and I are not alive.
We are two painted shells of eminence
Carried by two dead men. Because we move,
And breathe, and say a few complacent words
With tongues that are afraid to say our thoughts,
We think we are alive. But we are dead."

Caiaphas laughed: "Small wonder, Nicodemus,
That you conceal your death in some such rag
As that there on the floor when you go calling

[3]

On carpenters at night. How strong, I wonder,
With his assumptions and assurances,
Must a man be to be a carpenter
And honor your condescension without laughing."

"My fears and vanities are confessed. He smiled,
If that will comfort you, and then assured me
That he had more than once himself been driven
Not only to expediency, but hiding.
Yes, Caiaphas, good men like you and me
Have driven this man, if he be man, to vanish
Beyond the laws that hate him."

                                        "Why not say
Beyond the laws he hates, and done with it?
What's wrong with them? Would his be any
        better?
Our laws and Caesar's are enough, God knows,
To keep the safest of us occupied
With not forgetting them. This man is mad.
Believe me, Nicodemus, he is mad,
Or such an overflowing charlatan
As never was before. I have not heard him,
But waves of his high language have made echoes
All through Jerusalem. Beware of him,
I say to you, and stay at home o' nights.
I can see peril waiting, Nicodemus,
For this man—and for you, if you pursue him.
I am not given, or over much, to meddling,
But if you love him and would tell him so,

[4]

Tell him his home is not Jerusalem,
And hasten him away. You have the power
And place to save him. Save him, and you save
    more.
If he is what your folly says he is,
Why should he hide from powerless things of
    earth
Like us, who cannot hurt him? What strength is
    ours
To injure him? What can we do to him?
No, the whole story shakes. It's like a house
That creaks too soon—one that he might have
    built
When at his trade."

        "You may destroy his body,
Which is an instrument whereon the spirit
Plays for a time—and not for a long time,
He tells me. He must hold it as he may
From harm till there is no more use for it.
Meanwhile he is a man, with a man's end
Awaiting him. There is no fear in him,
But for the blindness that is ours who fear him."

"I am no more than man," said Caiaphas,
No longer smiling. "But I do not fear him;
And saving your regard, I am not blind.
Whether or not I am the painted shell
Of something dead, requires a contemplation.
I had not thought so, and had not been told

[5]

Until you spoke. Your vocal ornaments
Are not all complimentary this evening.
Are they the carpenter's?"

                    "No, they are mine,"
Said Nicodemus briefly, with a sigh.
"And they are past retraction or improvement.
You may forget them, but I'll not unsay them;
And spoken words that are unsaid are said
Only a little louder than at first.
No, Caiaphas; we are dead, and we are blind;
And worse than either, we are both afraid.
You don't like that."

                    "I treasure it so little,"
Caiaphas answered, rather quietly,
"That from another I might not receive it
Without a word in kind. But you are mad;
You and your carpenter are mad together,
And God sees what's to come. My office owes
A few indulgences and obligations
Even to madness, and I'll say no more—
No more than one more warning, Nicodemus,
That you provision your seditious prophet
Out of Jerusalem, and with no lost time."

"In God's name, Caiaphas," cried Nicodemus,
Rising and holding out his hands as if
To clutch two hands unseen, "is one poor string
The sum of all your music, and one word

[6]

Your only song? Because you are afraid,
Must you see nothing in the world but fear?
There is no fear in this man, Caiaphas.
He shuns a little while a coming death,
Which he foresees, that you and I may live;
And your fond warning now that I may save him
Is like a child's unwillingness to read
A book of easy letters that are life,
Because they are new letters, and not death.
You are a priest of death, not knowing it.
There is no life in those old laws of ours,
Caiaphas; they are forms and rules and fears,
So venerable and impressive and majestic
That we forget how little there is in them
For us to love. We are afraid of them.
They are the laws of death; and, Caiaphas,
They are the dead who are afraid of dying.
So do not say again that I may save
This man from death. There is no death for him."

"There may be something comfortingly like it,
If he is here too long," said Caiaphas;
"And I may soon be weary, Nicodemus,
Of hearing you repeat that I'm afraid.
The laws that were our fathers' laws are right
For me, and I can see no death in them,
Save death itself—which is the only death
I know. I know it, and I do not fear it;
Or not more than another. Only the mad
May welcome it, so long as life is better.

[7]

Have you a finger to lay on a law
Of ours that says to us we shall be mad?"

"No, Caiaphas; I'm not saying that we are mad.
I'm saying that we are dying while we are dead.
He tells me of light coming for the world,
And of men loving darkness more than light.
He is the light; and we, who love the dark
Because our fathers were at home in it,
Would hound him off alone into the hills
And laugh to see that we were rid of him.
In darkness we might see as much as that,
Not seeing what we were doing for ourselves
In doing ill for him. He will not die,
Though he find death where we have driven him.
The pity and waste of it is our not living,
With life so near us, and to take as ours,
Like shining fruit from an undying tree.
The fruit may fall, and we may crush the pulp
And blood of it, but it will not be dead.
It will replenish and increase itself
Immortally, because it is alive—
As even the lowly are, who love him first.
The lowly are the first inheritors
Of his report, the first acknowledgers
Of his reward—having no fame to lose,
No brief and tinsel perquisite of pomp,
Or profitable office, to renounce.
They are not politicians, Caiaphas,
Like you and me, who tremble when we step

An ell's length from the middle of the road;
They are not sceptred slaves of precedent
And privilege, who must buy their breath of life
With fears and favors and hypocrisies
That would, if recognized, make honor sick.
I say this, Caiaphas; for I have heard you
Citing the riff-raff that he feeds with words,
Telling them words are food till they believe it.
You have not heard and tasted them to know,
Or not to know, the food that lives in them
And quickens them till they are words no longer,
But are the Word. We tenants of high places
Are too high now to hear them, or to see
From where we are the inevitable harvest
Of this eternal sowing. Come with me,
But once, to see and hear him, Caiaphas;
Or, to be more courageous than I am,
Be once an item in the multitude,
And let yourself inquire, for once, how much
The lowliest, in his primal composition,
Would look, if you were God, like Caiaphas.
You don't like that, but there's a time for man
When he must speak, or die, or follow himself
To deserts where men starve and are forgotten.
I could starve here as well, and hate myself,
No doubt, a little harder for so doing.
I could sit starving in these noble robes,
As you have called them in your pleasantry,
But they would not be noble—not for me.
Truth is a sword of air cleaving the air,

[9]

Sometimes, to make it bleed; and here am I,
Armed, you would fancy, with a sword like that.
You smile to see me strike, drawing no blood—
Though blood may follow, and may God say
     whose;
And all so needlessly and against fate,
Except it be his fate that his worn body
Shall perish that he may live. So many have died
Before their work has lived that one more dying
Will not be new on earth; and this man's dying
Will not be death. What has truth done to us
That we must always be afraid of it,
As of a monster with a shape unknown
To man, prowling at night and breathing fire?
The truth is not like that; we are like that—
Or would be so if we were not so little.
Not all Jerusalem creeping in one skin
Would make a monster for this man to fear.
One fiery word of truth would pierce and frighten
Jerusalem then as now. We are afraid,
Caiaphas; and our flawed complacency
Is a fool's armor against revelation.
Why must we turn ourselves away from it?
If you and I together should stand with him,
For all to see, who knows what we should see!"

"We might see stones flying to find our heads,
For one thing, Nicodemus. You are mad.
Say to your carpenter that he is mad,
Or say what else you will. Take him away

While there is time, and hide him where the law
May lose him, or forget him. Telling you this,
I'm trying to say that a long suffering priest
May love a madman who has been a friend."

"Caiaphas, you are sorry to say that,
But will not own your sorrow, or your fear.
When sorrow hides itself in sophistry,
It might as well be scorn. I should have known.
I should have gone alone to my cold house
That will be colder for my coming here.
God knows what ails us in Jerusalem.
You cannot wash the taste of your misgivings
Away with wine, or rub the fear of them
Out of your face with an unquiet finger.
There's no security in a subterfuge
Where truth is marked a madness. I am not mad,
Unless a man is mad who brings a light
For eyes that will not open. I have been
A burden for your patience, Caiaphas.
I shall not come again."

                    " Yes, many a time,
I trust, and always welcome, Nicodemus.
When this absurdity has overblown
Its noise, and is an inch of history
That a few may remember, you will come.
There is a covenant that has not changed,
And cannot change. You will not go from us
For a mad carpenter; and as for him,

[11]

I am afraid for him unless you save him.
You may do that, but he will not save you—
As you would say it; for you are one of us,
And you will save yourself at the last hour;
And you will be as wary of Messiahs
Henceforth as I am. You may take yourself
Alone to him at night and feast with him
On dreams till you are drunk with his evangel,
And when your frenzied head is clear again,
You will rejoice, like a man dug from ruin,
To find the sun and stars, and the old laws,
Unfailing and unchanged and firm as ever.
You and your carpenter, while you have eyes,
Will not be seen as man and man together
Where there is daylight in Jerusalem.
Some things are not, and this is one of them.
When he is chained, or stoned, or crucified,
As like enough he will be if you let him,
You and your sorrow may be seen, too late,
Mourning where safety and necessity
Have buried him. But you will never be seen
With him beside you in Jerusalem.
I know you, Nicodemus."

                  Nicodemus
Trembled and held his cloak with clutching hands
As if it were his life. "Safety, you say?
Necessity, you say? Panic, I say!
Panic, and ancestors, and desperation!
Rabbits and rats! God help me, Caiaphas,

If I am what you see. If you are right,
I am not worth my name."

"As one of us,"
Caiaphas answered, and his words were calm—
"As one of us, I see you, Nicodemus,
True to our laws and hearts, and to our God,
Who chastened even Moses when he faltered,
And held him out of Canaan. Am I right?
Why, surely I am right. I am always right.
If I were wrong, I should not be a priest."

Caiaphas rubbed his hands together slowly,
Smiling at Nicodemus, who was holding
A black robe close to him and feeling it
Only as darkness that he could not see.
All he could see through tears that blinded him
To Caiaphas, to himself, and to all men
Save one, was one that he had left alone,
Alone in a bare room, and not afraid.

SISERA

From Taanach to Harosheth, by the river,
Barak had driven Sisera and his thousands
Till there were only a last few of them
Alive to feel, while there was time to feel,
Jehovah's hand and Israel's together,
Smiting invincibly. A slave of Canaan
For twenty years, now Israel was a slave
No more; and by the waters of Megiddo,
King Jabin's army was a picture drawn
Of men who slept. Sisera felt the dead
Behind him, and he knew the sound of death
Pursuing him—a sound that sang no hope
Or mercy for the few that were alive
Of Israel's enemy, and the last alive
That were to sleep that day, and for so long
As to be loved and trumpeted no more
By time and man than all who are forgotten.

Sisera, soon to see himself alone
Among the slain, or soon as one of them
To see not even himself left of his host,
Suddenly from his chariot, to rough ground,
Leapt as an animal from a flying cage

That plunged and rocked and staggered might
    have leapt,
Blindly, to wild escape and a short freedom.
Prone for a moment on hard earth he lay,
Bruised and amazed to find himself unbroken,
And with a quicker leap was up again,
And running—running as he believed no manner
Of man had run before—to the one place
He knew that might receive him yet and save him.
Heber the Kenite had no world to lose
Or win with either side, and was not fighting.
He was in Canaan frequently, moreover,
King Jabin's guest and friend; and his wife Jael
Was Jabin's adoration and desire,
And Sisera's despair. She frightened men
With her security, and she maddened them
With dark hot beauty that was more than woman's,
And yet all woman—or, as Jabin said
To Heber, enviously, perhaps all women
In one. If Sisera's fear remembered now
That there was more of Israelite in Jael
Than Canaanite or Kenite, he was running
Too fast and furiously and ruinously
For memories to be following him so far
As to the tents of Heber, where he prayed
For Jael and sanctuary. Her smile would save
A captain, as her frown would blast a king,
If she but willed it so. Sisera's feet
Flew as he thought of that, and his thought flew
Before him like a promise that he followed,

And followed flying. For an insane hour
He flew, and for another, and for a third,
And then fell helpless at the feet of Jael,
Who smiled at him unseen—which was as well
For Sisera; for her smile would save no captains,
Or none today.

         "If this comes out of Canaan
For me to save, then Israel must be free,"
She thought; and a thought slowly filled her heart
With music that she felt inflaming her
Deliriously with Deborah's word fulfilled.
Again she smiled, and went for cloths and water
To wash his heated face and his closed eyes,
Which, having seen her and been sure of her,
Saw nothing else until he felt the touch
Of her cool fingers and of her warm breath,
Incredible and together. His eyes opened
And found hers over them, shining at him
With a protection in them that he feared
Was too much like a mother's.

         "Speak," she said,
"And tell me who has fallen in this battle,
And who fares well. We Kenites are peace-lovers,
Not mixed with either camp—yet we must know.
Tell me, and sleep."

         "Yes, if you let me drink,"
He whispered, "I will tell you. Let me drink,
Or let me die. Let me die here with you,

If I must die. Not many of us are left
To die. This day is Israel's. Let me drink,
Or let me die. Let me die here with . . ."

                                       "No,"
She said, and smiled at him mysteriously.
"We are alive; and while we live—who knows?"
He reached with a blind hand for one of hers,
And held it while she said, "No, you must drink,"
And smiled: "Is there in Israel or in Canaan
A bowl of sleep like this for one so weary
As you? I have seen weariness before,
But never a man so made of weariness
That he shall not be flesh and bone again
Till sleep has made him so. Is it not cool
And healing as you feel it on your tongue,
And in your throat, and through you every-
    where—
Like life itself? It is the milk of life
That you are drinking. It will make you leap
Like a new lion when you are awake.
Yes, when you are awake. Now, now, my friend,
Now is your time to sleep."

                        "Before I sleep,
Hear this," he said: "There will come after me
Some ravening fiend of Israel to destroy me.
They will have nothing left of us alive.
For twenty years they have worn Canaan's yoke,
And always, in their dreams have known Jehovah,

[17]

Still watching them. They have believed in him;
And their belief will be the end of me—
Unless you say to them no man of Canaan
Has crossed your sight this day. If I say this
Asleep, or still awake, I am not here.
No man was here . . . No man . . ."

                                          "No, Sisera,"
She said with lips that moved without a sound,
"No man was here that will depart from here,
Except as weary meat for scavengers.
Was that what you were saying? It must have
    been,
For that was what I heard." She waited, crouch-
    ing,
And watched him with exalted eyes of triumph
That were not any longer woman's eyes,
But fixed and fierce and unimagined fires
Of death alive in beauty and burning it.
"No, Sisera; when they come, if they do come,
No man will be awaiting them. No man
Is here today who has not seen his last
Of Israel, and feared all there is for him
To fear of Israel. You are asleep
As only trust and weariness together
Makes a man sleep; and you will not feel this."
She laid an eager finger on his temple,
And pressed it, satisfied. Still watching him,
She moved away; and searching among shadows,

Found all she sought. "No, Sisera," she said,
Crooning above his face like a mad mother,
"There is no fear of Israel, or of earth,
Or of men living on earth, or things not men,
That you need fear today, or more tomorrow.
When they come here for you and say to me,
'Where is he?' I shall say, 'He is not here.
All that is here is yours. Take it away.'
See, Sisera! See what I have found for you.
Here is a nail as long as a man's life—
And sharp as death; and here is a brave hammer.
I found them there in the dark, where I remem-
    bered
Seeing them once. We had all best remember
Things we have seen, for soon or late we need
    them.
So, Sisera!"

       Slowly she drew away
The pillow she had lent his head to lie on,
And left his head lying sidewise on the floor.
Still crouching, she surveyed him, saying softly,
"So this is Canaan, who for twenty years
Believed that he was more than Israel!
Who is he now? What is he, Sisera?
You will not answer; for where Canaan sleeps
This day and night, there will be sleep indeed.
I can see thousands of you lying quiet;
And one will be one more."

The nail, sure-driven,
Transfixed a silent head that would not move
When she would see its face. And with him there,
What was a face? She had seen Sisera's face
Before; and it was no more Sisera now
Than were his fingers or his feet, she thought.
A face was not a man; and a man dead
Was less, or so it looked, than was a nail.
And she had driven the nail to make him dead,
For Deborah to celebrate, and for Barak
To see, and for all Israel to see.
Her life within her body was like fire—
A fire that healed in her the wrongs and sorrows
Of Israel sold in Canaan to a king
Who made a sport of his malignity,
And Sisera's; and now Sisera was dead.
All Israel would be told in a few hours
That Sisera was dead. And Deborah then
Would say to Barak: "The Lord's will be done!
Jael has killed Sisera—sing!—sing to the Lord!"

Still crouching over him, and watching him
Like an avenging image, she could hear
The coming sound of horses, and soon with it,
Confirming it, a murmur of men talking.
"Barak!" she told her heart; and her heart said,
"Barak!" And Jael arose in her rejoicing.
Outside she saw them, Barak and his men,
Who had known where to come. With arms aloft,
And eyes afire with triumph and thanksgiving,

She stood awaiting Barak. "Yes, he is here,"
She said; "and he is yours for no more seeking.
He will not fly away from you again."

"Hardly, if he is here," said Barak, halting.
He smiled at her with battle-heated eyes,
And met the fire of hers with admiration,
Mingled with weariness and victory,
And with a searching wonder. Then a spasm
Of silent laughter shook him and his voice:
"If he is here, you must have promised him
More than a man may give to make him stop.
We might have seized him, if necessity
Had said we must, and we might have him now
To count with his lost thousands; but we knew
That Heber's tent would hold him, if such run-
 ning
As his might last until you took him in.
At first, and for some time, we only watched him;
And all the horses watched him. Never since man
Was born to run has there been such a running
As this of Sisera's here today in Canaan.
Children who are unborn will emulate it;
And aged men will rise up out of chairs,
Remembering Sisera, and sit down again.
There's not a curse's worth of Canaan left,
Nor more than Sisera left of Jabin's army;
And Sisera's only safety is between
Jehovah and a woman—which is good,
If Jael is the Lord's woman. Well, where is he?"

Jael, who had partly heard him, turned and said,
"Follow me, Barak. I will show him to you.
And you, having seen how quiet and safe he is,
Will praise me. I shall have praise of Israel,
And of Jehovah shall have praise and glory,
For this that I have done. Since I remember,
I have heard voices of high prophecy,
Telling me to fulfil myself with patience
And readiness against an untold hour.
Now is the hour. The chosen of the Lord
Are told, if they will hear; and when the Lord
Has need of them they serve him—as they must.
My way to serve him was magnificent,
And will be praised for ever . . . See him,
    Barak!
Tell Deborah what you saw. Tell Deborah
That he is dead! Tell her that he is dead!
Tell her that everything that she foretold
Has come to pass. Tell her that he is dead!"

Barak, abrupt in battle, and in slaughter
Not subtle, till now had always made of war
A man's work, and of death attending it
An item necessary for a total.
So long as he should live, and live to fight
For Israel and for glory of the Lord,
Others would cease to live if they opposed him;
For that was the Lord's way, and Israel's way.
But this was not. He stared at Sisera's head,
Where the nail was, and slowly shook his own

Before he spoke: "I am not sure of this,"
He said, and looked at her uncertainly,
As if to ask for the first time, perhaps—
Whose hand held death for him. She who did this
Might one day flout her fealty to Jehovah
And lust for Baal. She might do anything.
So Barak only scowled and said to Jael,
"I am not sure of this. How was this done—
If he was not asleep?"

                "He was asleep,"
Jael said; and her eyes measured him with scorn
For one so artless and inquisitive;
"The Lord put him to sleep, and gave me strength
Of more than one small woman to destroy him.
So there he is. Tell Israel to rejoice.
Tell Deborah to rejoice. Tell Deborah
Where you saw Sisera dead, and bring her here
That she may see him. It was she who said
That Sisera was to die—and he is dead.
What is one man, or one man's way of dying,
So long as Israel has no more of him!"

Taut and erect she stood, and her possession
Bewildered Barak and astonished him
Into an awkward silence. All he did
Was to look down at Sisera, and once more
At Jael, not sure that he was looking at her.
At last he sighed, and made as if to throw
His hands away, having no use for them;

[23]

And having sighed again, he said to Jael,
"A world that holds so much for men to know
Must have been long in making. The Lord pon-
    dered
More than six days, I think, to make a woman.
The book of woman that has troubled man
So long in learning is all folly now.
I shall go home tonight and make another.
The wisest man alive, wherever he is,
Is not so wise that he has never wondered
What women do when they are left together,
Or left alone." He stood with folded arms
And with shut jaws, gazing at Sisera's head,
And at the driven nail piercing his head.
Scowling and thoughtful, he considered them
In silence, and then said, after some time,
"The tiger's wife, we're told. . . . I've all to
    learn.
Is this what women do?"

          "Tell Deborah,"
Jael answered, as if answering a voice
Farther away than Barak's, "that I killed him.
Tell Deborah, who foretold it, that a woman,
A woman filled with God, killed Sisera
For love of Israel, and that you have seen him,
As he is now, with no more harm in him.
Tell Deborah this right hand of mine was God's
That hammered in the nail—while Sisera slept.
Tell her my hand was God's that held the nail—

While Sisera slept. Say Jael and God together
Made Sisera what you see. Sing to the Lord,
Barak! And say to Deborah, 'Jael says,
Sing to the Lord!' For now there shall be peace
In Israel, and a sound of women singing—
A sound of children singing, and men singing—
All singing to the Lord! There is no king
In Canaan who is king of Israel now!
This day is ended—and there is no King
In Israel but the Lord! Sing to the Lord!
Let Israel see the dark of a day fading,
And sing!—praising a day that has an end.
Let Israel see the light of a day breaking,
And sing!—hailing a day that has a dawn.
Sing to the King of Israel her Thanksgiving!
Sing to the King of Glory! Sing to the Lord!"

TOUSSAINT L'OUVERTURE

(Chateau de Joux, 1803)

Am I alone—or is it you, my friend?
I call you friend, but let it not be known
That such a word was uttered in this place.
You are the first that has forgotten duty
So far as to be sorry—and perilously,
For you—that I am not so frozen yet,
Or starved, or blasted, that I cannot feel.
Yes, I can feel, and hear. I can hear something
Behind me. Is it you? There is no light,
But there's a gray place where a window was
Before the sun went down. Was there a sun?
There must have been one; for there was a light,
Or sort of light—enough to make me see
That I was here alone. Was I forgotten?
I have been here alone now for three days,
Without you, and with nothing here to eat
Or drink; and for God knows how many months,
Or years, before you came, have I been here—
But never alone so long. You must be careful,
Or they will kill you if they hear you asking
Questions of me as if I were a man.

[26]

I did not know that there was anything left
Alive to see me, or to consider me,
As more than a transplanted shovelful
Of black earth, with a seed of danger in it—
A seed that's not there now, and never was.
When was I dangerous to Napoleon?
Does a perfidious victor fear the victim
That he has trapped and harassed? No, he hates
    him.
The only danger that was ever in me
Was food that his hate made to feed itself.
There lives in hate a seed more dangerous
To man, I fear, than any in time's garden
That has not risen to full stalk and flower
In history yet. I am glad now for being
So like a child as to believe in him
As long as there was hope. And what was hope?
Hope was a pebble I brought here to play with,
And might as well have dropped into the ocean
Before there was a bitter league of it
Between me and my island. It was well
Not to do that. Not that it matters now.

My friend, I do not hear you any longer.
Are you still there? Are you afraid to speak?
You are the first thing fashioned as a man
That has acknowledged me since I came here—
To die, as I see now—with word or motion
Of one man in the same world with another;
And you may be afraid of saying to me

Some word that hurts your tongue. Have they
    invented
A last new misery fit for the last days
Of an old sick black man who says tonight
He does not think that he shall have to live
Much longer now? If there were left in me
A way to laugh, I might as well be laughing
To think of that. Say to Napoleon
That he has made an end of me so slowly,
And thoroughly, that only God Almighty
Shall say what is to say. And if God made him,
And made him as he is, and has to be,
Say who shall answer for a world where men
Are mostly blind, and they who are the blindest
Climb to cold heights that others cannot reach,
And there, with all there is for them to see,
See nothing but themselves. I am not one
To tell you about that, for I am only
A man destroyed, a sick man, soon to die;
A man betrayed, who sees his end a ruin,
Yet cannot see that he has lived in vain.
Though he was crushed and humbled at the last
As things are that are crawling in man's way,
He was a man. God knows he was a man,
And tells him so tonight. Another man
Mixed fear with power and hate and made of it
A poison that was death, and more than death,
And strangled me to make me swallow it—
And here I am. I shall not be here long
To trouble you; and I shall not forget

Your seeing in me a remnant of mankind,
And not a piece of God's peculiar clay
Shaped as a reptile, or as a black snake.
A black man, to be sure; and that's important.

I cannot tell you about God, my friend,
But in my life I have learned more of men
Than would be useful now, or necessary,
If a man's life were only a man's life.
Sometimes it is, or looks to be, no better
Than a weed growing to be crushed or cut,
Or at the most and best, or worst, to live
And shrivel and slowly die and be forgotten.
Others are not like that; and it appears
That mine was not. Mine was a million lives,
And millions after them. Why am I here!
What have I done to die in a cold hole
In a cold land that has no need of me?
Men have been mightier than in doing this thing
To me, I think. Yet who am I to say it?
An exile, buried alive in a cold grave
For serving man, as men may still remember.
There are diseased and senseless ways of hate
That puzzle me—partly because I'm black,
Perhaps, though more because of things that are,
And shall be, and for God may say how long.

Hear me, and I will tell you a strange thing—
Which may be new and of an interest
To many who may not know so much of me

[29]

As even my name until my name shall have
A meaning in this world's unhappy story.
Napoleon cannot starve my name to death,
Or blot it out with his. There is an island
Where men remember me; and from an island
Surprising freight of dreams and deeds may come,
To make men think. Is it not strange, my friend—
If you are there—that one dishonored slave,
One animal owned and valued at a price,
One black commodity, should have seen so early
All that I saw? When I filled sight with action,
I could see tyranny's blood-spattered eyes
That saw no farther, laughing at God and fate,
Than a day's end, or possibly one day more,—
Until I made them see. Was it not strange?
Drivers and governors of multitudes
Must be more than themselves, and have more
    eyes
Than one man's eyes, or scorn will bury them,
Or leave them worse uncovered; and time will pass
    them
Only to kick their bones. I could see that;
And my prophetic eyes, where God had fixed them
In this black face, could see in front of them
A flaming shambles of men's ignorance
Of all that men should know. I could see farther;
And in a world far larger than my island
Could see the foul indifferent poison wreaking
Sorrow and death and useless indignation
On millions who are waiting to be born;

And this because the few that have the word
Are mostly the wrong few in the wrong places.
On thrones or chairs of state too high for them,
Where they sit swollen or scared, or both, as may be,
They watch, unseen, a diligent see-saw
Played by their privileged and especial slaves
On slippery planks that shake and smell of blood
That flows from crushed and quivering backs and
    arms
Of slaves that hold them up. There are more slaves
Than have yet felt or are to feel, and know it,
An iron or a lash. This will go on
Until more slaves like me, and more, and more,
Throw off their shackles and make swords of them
For those to feel who have not felt before,
And will not see. It will go on as long
As men capitulate who feel and see,
And men who know say nothing. If this means
It must go on for always—well I have done
All that one man—one black man, I should say—
Could do against a madness and a system
And a malicious policy, all rotten
With craft and hate. It will be so again:
Humanity will hear the lash of scorn
And ignorance again falling on hope,
And hearing it will feel it. Ignorance,
Always a devil, is a father of devils
When it has power and fire and hate to play with,
And goes down with the noise of its own house
Falling, always too late to save itself,

Because it has no eyes. That's power, my friend.
If you are sorry to be born without it,
Be sorry for something else, and answer me:
Is power a breaking down of flesh and spirit?
Is foresight a word lost with a lost language?
Is honor incomprehensible? Is it strange,
That I should sit here and say this to you—
Here in the dark? . . . Nothing to eat or drink,
Nothing to do but die? This is not right. . . .
Hear me, and I will tell you what I saw.

Last night I saw Napoleon in hell.
He was not dead, but I knew where he was,
For there was fire and death surrounding him
Like red coals ringed around a scorpion
To make him sting himself rather than burn.
Napoleon burned. I saw his two hands flaming;
And while I saw him I could see that hate
For me was still alive in his blind eyes.
I was no happier for the sight of him,
For that would not help me; and I had seen
Too much already of crime and fire at work
Before I made an end of it—for him
To make of peace a useless waste and fury.
I have not yet gone mad, for I have known
That I was right. It seems a miracle,
Yet I am not so sure it is a mercy
That I have still my wits and memories
For company in this place. I saw him there,
And his hands that were flaming with a fire

They caught from the same fire that they had
 lighted.
So fire will act, sometimes, apparently.
Well, there he was, and if I'm not in error,
He will be there again before he dies;
And that will not be medicine here for this.
There is no cure for this, except to die,
And there is nothing left that is worth hating—
Not even the hate of him that kills with hate.
Is it that I am weak—or am I wise?
Can a black man be wise? He would say not.
Having his wisdom, he would have to say it
To keep his hate alive; and without that
He would soon hate the sound of his own name.
Prisons have tongues, and this will all be told;
And it will not sound well when men remember.

Where are you now? Is this another night?
Another day—and now another night?
I do not hear you any more, my friend.
Where are you? Were you ever here at all?
I have been here alone now for too long.
They will not let you come to me again
Until you come to carry a dead man—
I see it now—out of this cold and darkness
To a place where black and white are dark together.
Nothing to eat or drink—nothing to do
But wait, and die. No, it will not sound well.
Where are you now, my friend? I cannot hear you;
I cannot feel you. Are you dead, perhaps?

[33]

I said to you it would be perilous
Not to remember that I'm not a man,
But an imprudent piece of merchandise
To buy and sell—or this time rather to steal;
To catch and steal, and carry from my island
To France, and to this place. And in this place,
Is it not strange, my friend, for me to see
So clearly, and in the dark, more than he sees
Who put me here—as I saw long ago
More than a man could do, till it was done?
Yes, it is done, and cannot be undone.
I know, because I know; and only those
Whose creed and caution has been never to know
Will see in that no reason . . . Yes, I know,
My friend, but I do not know where you are.
If you are here, help me to rise and stand
Once more. I cannot sleep. I cannot see.
Nothing to eat or drink—nothing to see
But night. Good night, my friend—if you are here.

Nothing to see but night—and a long night,
My friend. I hear you now. I hear you moving,
And breathing. I can feel you in the dark,
Although I cannot see you. . . . Is this night?
Or is it morning! No, it is not night—
For now I see. You were a dream, my friend!
Glory to God, who made a dream of you,
And of a place that I believed a prison.
There were no prisons—no Napoleons.
I must have been asleep for a long time.

Now I remember. I was on a ship—
A ship they said was carrying me to France.
Why should I go to France? I must have slept,
And sailed away asleep, and sailed on sleeping.
I am not quite awake; yet I can see
White waves, and I can feel a warm wind coming—
And I can see the sun! . . . This is not France—
This is a ship; and France was never a ship.
France was a place where they were starving me
To death, because a black man had a brain.
I feel the sun! Now we are going faster—
Now I see land—I see land and a mountain!
I see white foam along a sunny shore—
And there's a town. Now there are people in it,
Shouting and singing, waving wild arms at me,
And crowding down together to the water!
You know me—and you knew that I was coming!
O you lost faces! My lost friends! My island!
You knew that I was coming. . . .

                                    You are gone.
Where are you gone? Is this the night again?
I cannot see you now. But you are there—
You are still there. And I know who is here.

PONCE DE LEON
(HAVANA, 1521)

In Florida, the fair land he had named
In admiration of its many blossoms,
And for its opulence of promises,
De Leon, with an arrow in his thigh,
Lay stricken on the shore of his new world,
Cursing it while he groaned and heard the sound
Of water washing always on the sand.
Around him, in a circle, all his men,
Burning in armor hardly to be borne,
Stood sweltered in defeat, and in despair
Of what was next to do; and high above them,
Blazing as if to melt them and their master,
The tropic sun rose higher. A look of thanks
For their protection and their loyalty,
Was all he had for them while arrows flew
From ambush, like fierce insects, and found iron
Instead of flesh.

          Only when they were all
Afloat again, and safe away from arrows,
Was there more time for words: "If this thing
    here

Is venomous, you had better pray for me,
For you may do no more. I know its method,"
He said, and scanned the arrow that he held
Now in his fingers. "Take me away from here.
There is a man of learning in Havana,
A sage and a physician, an old man,
Whose ways are famous. Men have said of him
That he reads all that we have written on us
Of what we are within, and has a genius
In all obscure things that are physical,
To make them right and well. It may be so,
But I am bitten deep; and I am older
Than a man is who tames a wilderness
For sport of being the first. I should have known
Before that my home now is in my house,
Which I have left behind me, and may see. . . .
Well, we shall see."

                     Time and a silent voyage
Brought a slow ship and its unhappy freight
At last into the harbor of Havana,
Where the man was who might explore and heal
De Leon's wound, if there was healing for it
In mortal knowledge . . . And when all was done
That might, for even the most magnificent
Of invalids, be feasible, the physician
Would only smile and say, "You are too old,
My lord, for such a perilous game as this.
Have you not fought and toiled and found enough
For one man's appetency, without this?

Why has a man a fair wife, and a house
Of state, and famous wealth, and a grand name,
If he must only sail away from them
And let one vicious hidden angry savage
Do this? Is Midas less than a mosquito?
God save you men of action, who will never
Be done with acting. Be a child again
In spirit, and our Saviour will reward you;
But if you be a child again in deeds,
He may be overtaxed, and leave to nature
Those who offend it. He left nature with us
That we should recognize it and observe it,
And through it find a wiser way to grace
Than we are finding yet."

        De Leon, lying
In a wide room that was as cool as rooms
Could be in Cuba, said with a twist of pain
That might have been a smile, "I see the drift
Of your evasions, or believe I do;
For I have been a sinner in this world
Of sin too long, and heard too many lies,
And told too many, to receive as healing
Your playful way of covering a last hope
With colors that I fear are mostly made
Of dust and water."

        "You are making words
Into a poultice for your pain, my lord;
And I have seen strong men who have done less,

And with less fortitude. If speech is hard,
Lie with your eyes closed for a little while,
And let some valorous pictures of yourself
And your performances inspirit you
More than I may. To you that shake the world
And change it, and have never enough of it,
We that are only scholars, or physicians,
Are so like books with faces, books that walk,
That we must let you do our living for us,
And thereby be the mightier. You are mighty;
So close your eyes, and let the past come back."

"There is too much of it that will come back,
My friend, whether I close my eyes or not.
There are no valorous pictures of myself
That will inspirit me, as you will have it,
And there are few of my performances
That are good memories, or good food for souls.
You say the arrow was not venomous,
But that another venom has come in
To make my wound a flame and a damnation.
You know, not I. I don't know that it matters
What fire it is that burns. For I am burning,
Burning; and this poor fuel that I am
May not last long. Unless the fire goes out,
I shall weigh more as ashes than as man.
Doctor, are you my friend? You say you are,
And your eyes are an answer. If you are,
How long have I to live?"

"Could I say that,"
The old man answered, partly with his shoulders,
"I might be questioned as an evil spirit,
And burned alive. Is it not God's first mercy
To suffering man that he shall not know when?
Why do you ask for more than you would know?
Will you in your distress, and your disaster,
Forget what you have made of these wild islands,
Or what your royal mother, royal Spain,
Will say of you? Nor Spain alone, my lord;
For there's a world will say it. So take heart
Of glory, and be glorious over pain.
Your deeds are yours, and what is yours is you.
And what of all the gates that you have opened,
With your name shining over them in gold?
Is there dominion without victory,
My lord? And is there victory without price?"

"Doctor, I see so little to deceive me
That your deceit is innocence. Forgive me—
I mean your kindness to a stricken man,
Who sees more gates with his name over them
In blood now than in gold. Or why not both?
When were they not blood-brothers and allies
In this 'dominion' and this 'victory'
Of yours? Are they my comfort and reward?
Dominion, is it? There was more of it
In one small arrow than there was in me.
You know; and all your skill and all your science
Will give me only words to make me well."

[40]

The old man smiled: "I say to you again,
Unlock the casket of your memories
And gaze on what is in it. You will see
Jewels of conquest there, rich and intact,
And indestructible; and you will see
Treasures of effort and accomplishment
Waiting for time's account."

                           "Yes, time's account,"
De Leon answered, "will indeed appraise them.
The only jewels of mine that I would see
Today are my wife, Ines, and her children.
I left them all, a man too old for folly,
For a fool's voyage to find in Florida
God knows what sort of gain. Jealous of time,
Or Cortes, I must have a world unknown
To conquer and call mine. When does a man
Become his years, and see that these new doings
Are not for men at rest and in the shade,
With deeds enough behind them to remember,
And to be sorry for? I practised evil
Sufficient for one man's alacrity
In Boriquen, or call it Puerto Rico,
And should have been content. Now I can see,
And read the wisdom of a wiser God
Who hid from me that fountain I was after,
In a lost island that I never found,
That I might flourish always. Had I found it,
I might have walked with iron feet for ever
Over the maimed or slaughtered flesh and faces

Of those who trusted me. Are we the worst,
We Spanish, of all who might have been appointed
For the blind occupation and the ruin
Of this new land, or are we as we are
Because we are here first? Are the first always
The worst? Are they, being drunk with ignorance
And opportunity, by God's will ordained
And pampered for their ultimate undoing?
Does history say so? I am not a scholar,
And have not read so deeply as to know.
Meanwhile I fear me, and for proper cause,
There may stay after us, here in these islands,
A mortal odor that will smell of slaughter,
And will be slow to die, being death itself.
I wish to God that we who have done this
Had not forgotten time in our time-service."

The scholar shook his head, and laid his hand
Affectionately on De Leon's forehead.
"My lord, there is no hope in this you say,
    Although God knows there may be truth in it.
    Truth is not always hope; nor, as we learn,
    Is anguish always death. There are surprises.
    Listen, and you will hear a sound of hope
    In those slow waves below us on the shore.
    They break, and end; yet they are always there,
    And they are never ending. Do you hear them?"
De Leon sighed, glad for the touch he felt,
Cool on his forehead: "Doctor, your poor wallet
Of words has not much left in it for me.

[42]

Have you an ear so out of tune with truth
As to believe that there was ever a sound
Of hope in any waves on any shore?
My living hope is where you know it is,
And it is not in waves. Are you so dry
With desperation as to make me drink
The sound of water, saying there's life in it?
Here's water, at least, and not the sound of it;
And water warm as blood. Is God's whole world
Itself burning alive, as I am burning?
Your hand is cool, doctor; yet if those waves
Down there have any hope in them for you,
You are the father and mother of hope. For me,
They are the music of time's funeral,
Which is a long one, and appears to have
No end. My friend, your eyes accuse your tongue,
And they say truth to one whose place and fame
Are two delusions, founded and established
On tricks and treacheries and exterminations.
God!—must a man be looking at his grave
Before he sees of what his house is built
That he is leaving?"

     "No, no! You are speaking
As one of your despairing islanders,
Who sees extinction in a slow eclipse—
Until the shadow vanishes."

      "No, no,
My friend. And mine is a more potent no
Than yours, for I have memories, and my eyes

[43]

That see where yours do not. There was a land
Where destiny had been asleep for ages
Until I came to shake it, and my reign
Began. There was no going away from it,
Or leaving it unused, for time had spoken;
But there are farther seeing ways than ours
Of cutting nature's throat. I was the end
Of nature for those children of the earth,
Who hailed me as they would have hailed a god—
With joy and welcome, and with adoration.
They more than half believed that I was God,
Until I was revealed and was a devil—
Far worse than any of theirs; for theirs at least
Were native, and were understandable.
My ways were not so devilish, if you like,
If you insist, as were Ovando's ways
In Haiti, but I'll say no more for them.
You are a doctor of our minds and bodies;
You have read many books, and have left men
To die, knowing your knowledge could not save
    them—
Which is not much to know. To know yourself
Incarnate and inviolate in God's image,
You should be noble. You should be the flower
Of man, with a new world for you to ruin,
And ruin it, to see things that we have seen.
Then you and others like you, and like me,
Might see men drown themselves and hang them-
    selves,
And women leap with children from high cliffs,

Rather than see your faces any longer,
Or meet another sunrise. If they knew you
As a physician, and as one of us,
They might avoid you, or might be too sick
To care."

     "Oh, this is bitterness, my lord!
You may be feeling wounds you never made.
I have heard many legends of Ovando,
Of Roldan and of Esquival, and others,
And their extremities, but fewer of you
And yours. There may be gratitude unspoken
For you in some dark hearts, and silent thanks
For thoughts and acts that you may have for-
  gotten;
And you may still go back, and find them there."

De Leon smiled, and frowned—feeling a tear
Tickle his cheek. "There is no gratitude
Awaiting me, nor silent thanks, I fear,
Save in my house, where they may well be silent.
For I shall not go back—or not without
Some flags and cannon to say who is coming.
We noble knaves and worshipful bloodhounds
Must have processions and reverberations
When we are dead, or men may not believe
That we were noble. I shall be heard, not hear-
  ing
The sound my going makes. I only hope
When I am out of this, I shall not hear

[45]

Some cries, and other sounds, that I have heard
Above the music my renown has made
For my magnificence. I have heard sounds,
Doctor, not to be heard—not even in hell."

"You are saying this to me alone, my lord;
And you are wiser for not hiding it
Within you, to become another poison.
The marks that you are making on yourself
Are more the brand of a bad fellowship
And of a seething fever, drugged with gold,
I fancy, than of ingrained willing evil.
If we knew more of our self-clouded means
And privileges, I might say more of this.
Being man, I say no more—saving a word
Of thanks to God, and of congratulation
To man, for your not coming to your fountain."

De Leon smiled again: "I have said that,
My friend, and with no lightness of defeat,
Or cynical deliverance. I believe
There is a time for man that has been measured,
By a wise God, and measured mercifully.
When I asked that old woman from Luquillo,
Who came once to my house with a long story
Of water that would heal man of his years
And hold him here for ever, if she herself
Had tasted it, she laughed at me, and said,
'No, master, I am doing well without it.
But it is there, and I will send you there,

[46]

If you are sure that you are thirsting for it.
Be sure that you are sure. I have lived well
For more years than I need to live again,
And I don't want it.' I conceive suspicion,
Doctor, when I set out on that north voyage,
That I was looking more for a new land
That I had never seen, than for a fountain
That I should never find. I never found it;
And while you look at me, I am not sorry.
For there is peace and wisdom in your eyes,
And no fear for the end—which is worth more
To me now than all fountains. Tell me something.
Tell me—what does it mean?"

                          "Some of it means,
My lord," the old man answered, easily,
"That hidden voices are in some of us,
  And, when we least would hear them, whisper
      to us
That we had better go the other way.
And other voices are in some of us,
 Telling us to go on as we are going—
So long as we go sensibly and fairly,
And with a vigilance. There are voices also,
Saying that if this world is only this,
We are remarkable animate accidents,
And are all generated for a most
Remorseless and extravagant sacrifice
To an insatiate God of nothing at all—
Who is not mine, or yours. And there are voices

[47]

Coming so far to find us that I doubt
If you, my lord, have yet an ear to seize them.
They may be near you now, unrecognized,
If not unwelcome, and like unseen strangers
In a dark vestibule, saying in vain
That they are always there. You cannot listen
To more than you may hear; you cannot measure
More than is yours to comprehend."

       "No, doctor,"
De Leon said, holding his pain as hands
Of island slaves held fire, because they must,
"But you may see me lying here on this rack,
And pierce me with hot wires until I die.
Forgive me. All you say is excellent
For my nobility, but no cure for me.
What else I may have earned, I may know soon.
Now it will not be long."

     There was a pause
That was not hesitation. "No, it will not
Be long, my lord." The old man said it kindly,
And without sorrow, and without regret
That was revealed: "I shall soon follow you,
For I am old; too old to be afraid,
Or to care tragically where or when—
So long as there are voices."

      "There are voices,
Doctor, which I am glad you do not hear.
And I am glad your eyes are watching me.

[48]

They say more than you told me. Without them,
Your words might all have crumbled, or been lost
In that long sound down there of broken water,
Where you found hope. I can see more in them
Than I can see in all the sixty years
That I have lived. I don't say what it is;
I don't know what it is; and shall not ask—
So long as it is there. It may be voices."

"I doubt if they will hold or show so much
For you as that, my lord," the old man said;
"Though surely my old eyes, which have seen
        more
Than they will see again, or wish to see
Of this torn world and its infirmities,
Should have some wisdom in them by this time,
And some forbearance. There is no cry for haste,
Yet when you have revealed your memories
To your confessor, and have made your peace
With God, you will be wiser, and be done
With fear, which I see written on you still.
Your pain will then be less your enemy
Than fear is now. You do not look to me,
My lord, so black as you have drawn yourself
In your defeat. Ambition forgets time,
And opportunities are mighty forces;
And we are not omnipotent, or all-wise.
I am not very wise; but I am old,
And I shall follow you in a few years,
Or a few days—or I may go before you.

[49]

Our minutes are all arrows. If one strikes,
There is no balsam for it, and we go;
And Time has a last arrow for himself."

"Doctor, if you were God, I should believe you;
Since you are mortal, I can only thank you
For saying not too much truth. If I might live,
I might exalt you, and give you a name
Larger than mine. You would not care for that—
Or for my fountain. It was best for me,
And for all men, that I was not to find it.
Now let me say to God all that He knows
Of me that I may say. I hope He knows
A little more of me than I remember."

De Leon sighed, and felt the old man's hand
Cool on his forehead, as it was before,
And closed his eyes to be alone with pain.
Yet he was not alone, for the same eyes
Were there. He smiled, knowing them to be
    there,
And opened his to say that he was ready.

ANNANDALE AGAIN

Almost as if my thought of him
Had called him from he said not where,
He knocked. I knew him through the door,
And Annandale was waiting there.

Nothing of years or distances,
Or deserts that he may have ranged,
Betrayed him. He was Annandale,
The only man who never changed.

"Do as you must," he said, "and God
Will say that you have done no wrong.
Begin by disappointing me,
And ask where I have been so long.

"What matter's it where I have been,
Or on what mountain or what star?
All places are as much alike
As all men and all women are—

"How Annandale Went Out," published in *The Town Down the River*, 1910, is reprinted on page 60.

[51]

"Which is not much. The best of us
Are curiously unlike the worst;
And for some time, at any rate,
The last shall never be the first.

"Wherefore I leave them, having done
No harm to them, or none to show."—
There was no liking such a man;
You loved him, or you let him go.

"Dreamers who crave a common yoke
For bulls and ewes and elephants
May have it; and my having mine
May be a soothing circumstance

"For you and me, and for my wife;
I mean my new wife Damaris.
I'll tell you, if you must be told,
The sort of woman that she is.

"When Miriam died, my former wife,
I wept and said that all was done;
Yet even as long ago as then
My darkness had a smothered sun

"Behind it, trying to shine through.
More like a living voice of light
It was, than like the sun itself,
And my night was not wholly night.

"And my world was not wholly gone,
  As I had feared. Well, hardly so.
  I wonder we should learn to live,
  Where there's so much for us to know.

"For that, we don't. We live meanwhile;
  And then, with nothing learned, we die.
  God has been very good to him
  Whose end is not an asking why.

"But I'm astray, beginning ill
  To lose myself in setting out;
  It was my new wife Damaris
  That you were asking me about.

"Your interest was an innocence,
  And your concern was no surprise.
  Well, I have brought her home with me,
  And you may find her in my eyes.

"In general, there's no more to tell;
  Yet there's this in particular:
  She knows the way the good God made
  My fur to lie; and there you are.

"And that's enough; you know the rest.
  You know as much as I may learn,
  Should we go to the end of time
  Together, and through time return

"To now again. I should like that,
Ad infinitum. So you see
How graciously has fate prepared
A most agreeable trap for me.

"For where we stay because we must,
Prison or cage or sacrament,
We're in a trap. This world is one,
Obscurely sprung for our ascent,

"Maybe, till we are out of it,
And in another. Once I thought
My cage was dark; but there was light
To let me see that I was caught

"For always there, with Damaris
In the same cage. It's large enough
To hold as many as two of us,
With no constraint worth speaking of.

"The Keeper, who's invisible,
Reveals himself in many a sign,
To caution me that I shall read
And heed the benefits that are mine—

"I don't say hers. Still, if she likes
Her cage with me, and says it's home,
And sings in it, what shall I say
That you may not find wearisome?

[54]

"You doctors, who have found so much
   In matter that it's hardly there,
   May all, in your discomfiture,
   Anon be on your knees in prayer

"For larger presence of what is
   In what is not. Then you will see
   Why Damaris, who knows everything,
   Knows how to find so much in me.

"She finds what I have never found
   Before; and there's a fearsome doubt,
   Sometimes, that slumbers and awaits
   A day when Damaris finds out

"How much of undistinguished man
   There is in her new destiny.
   When she divines it, I shall not
   Be told, or not immediately—

"Nor ever, if I'm as amiable
   As her attention apprehends.
   I'm watching her, and hiding tight
   Within me several odds and ends

"Of insights and forbearances
   And cautious ways of being kind,
   That she has dropped like handkerchiefs,
   Conceivably for me to find.

"But one shall not acquire all this
At once, or so it would appear.
I've lain awake establishing
Her permutations in a year—

"Not always indispensable,
You say; and yet, for recompense,
Revealing, when it looks like rain,
A refuge of intelligence;

"Which, with all honor to the rest
That makes a cage enjoyable,
Is not the least of ornaments
That every woman may as well

"Inherit as an amulet
For disillusions unforeseen—
Assuming always that for her
May still be some that have not been.

"Meanwhile, perfection has a price
That humor always has to pay
With patience, as a man may learn
Of woman when she has her way.

"While Miriam lived, I made a book
To make another woman wise.
Blessed are they who are not born
Above instruction by surprise.

"But there was wisdom in it too;
  And there are times her eyes are wet
  With wonder that I should foresee
  So much of her before we met.

"Again, when her complexities
  Are restive, or she may have bruised
  An elbow on the bars of home,
  I may be for a time confused;

"But not for long. She gratifies
  A casual need of giving pain;
  And having drawn a little blood,
  She folds her paws and purrs again.

"So all goes well; and with our wits
  Awake, should go indefinitely—
  Sufficient without subterfuge,
  Harmonious without history.

"You'll find us cheerful prisoners
  Enough, with nothing to bewail.
  I've told you about Damaris;
  And I'll go home."—Poor Annandale!

  Poor Damaris! He did not go
  So far as home that afternoon.
  It may be they offended fate
  With harmonies too much in tune

[57]

For a discordant earth to share
Unslain, or it may just have been,
Like stars and leaves and marmosets,
Fruition of a force unseen.

There was a sick crash in the street,
And after that there was no doubt
Of what there was; and I was there
To watch while Annandale went out.

No pleasure was awaiting me,
And there would have been none for you;
And mine was the one light I had
To show me the one thing to do.

Sometimes I'll ask myself, alone,
The measure of her debt to me
If some of him were still alive,
And motionless, for her to see;

Sometimes I'll ask if Annandale,
Could he have seen so far ahead,
Had been so sure as I am now
Of more than all he might have said.

I'll ask, and ask, and always ask,
And have no answer; or none yet.
The gain that lives in woman's loss
Is one that woman may forget

For a long time. A doctor knows
The nature of an accident;
And Damaris, who knows everything,
May still be asking what it meant.

HOW ANNANDALE WENT OUT
(1910)

"They called it Annandale,—and I was there
To flourish, to find words, and to attend:
Liar, physician, hypocrite, and friend,
I watched him; and the sight was not so fair
As one or two that I have seen elsewhere:
An apparatus not for me to mend—
A wreck, with hell between him and the end,
Remained of Annandale. And I was there.

"I knew the ruin as I knew the man;
So put the two together, if you can,
Remembering the worst you know of me.
Now view yourself as I was, on the spot,—
With a slight kind of engine. Do you see?
Like this . . . You wouldn't hang me? I thought
    not."

THE SPIRIT SPEAKING
(CHRISTMAS, 1929)

As you are still pursuing it
　　As blindly as you can,
You have deformed and tortured it
　　Since ignorance began;
And even as you have mangled it,
　　The Letter has killed man.

Because a camel cannot well
　　Go through a needle's eye,
No jealous God has ever said
　　The son of man must die;
Only the God that you have made
　　Has mocked you from the sky.

No God has in his mightiness
　　Told you that love is fear;
And some of you, who are almost
　　Too mighty to be here,
May fancy that you are not so—
　　If only once a year.

[61]

As long as you contend with it
For longer fear and pain,
As always you have injured it
And angered it again,
A grief and a malevolence
The Letter will remain.

YOUNG GIDEON
(Judges, 6)

Young Gideon would have threshed his father's
    wheat
With no more words, and as obediently
As other sons were toiling in Manasseh,
Where toil was tribute and a vanity.

Another day would be another day
For Gideon now; and round him everywhere,
Whether he toiled or slept, there would be always
Eyes watching, and a presence of despair.

There were too many presences with eyes,
Invisible and alert; they were like fire,
Piercing his heart and brain, till anger made him
A slave without ambition or desire.

Why toil so long to feed a Midian mouth,
With shame his only wages? Why not make
Jehovah's wrath aware of one who feared him
Less than he feared dishonor for his sake?

[63]

If this was life, why not be done with life?
The means at hand was his, and his the choice.
So Gideon waited for the word within him,
Hearing it not. He heard instead the Voice.

The least of a small house in a poor land
Until today, he shook, and feared to raise
His eyes to see the common things around him
That looked as far off as old yesterdays.

He knew, and still he feared—as prisoners fear
The weariness of waking. Yet he knew;
He knew that his one doubt was a thing dying
Before it should be born. It was all true.

God found him young, and in his youth had found
Faith to mock knowledge, knowledge to mock fear.
Why then was he afraid if he feared nothing?
God knew his Gideons, and the way was clear.

He would have danced and sang there where he
    was,
With Israel pitying him, for all he cared.
Meanwhile he pitied Israel for not knowing
How many were soon to perish, or be spared.

Now that he knew the man that in himself
Had been a stranger, freedom, like a bell,
Sang through him; and he knew that while he
    trembled
His fear was only joy for Israel.

He trembled while he felt the Midian yoke
Releasing him; and there was in release
No fear, until a second morning found him
Fearing to find the dew upon the fleece.

THE PRODIGAL SON

You are not merry, brother. Why not laugh,
As I do, and acclaim the fatted calf?
For, unless ways are changing here at home,
You might not have it if I had not come.
And were I not a thing for you and me
To execrate in anguish, you would be
As indigent a stranger to surprise,
I fear, as I was once, and as unwise.
Brother, believe, as I do, it is best
For you that I'm again in the old nest—
Draggled, I grant you, but your brother still,
Full of good wine, good viands, and good will.
You will thank God, some day, that I returned,
And may be singing for what you have learned,
Some other day; and one day you may find
Yourself a little nearer to mankind.
And having hated me till you are tired
You will begin to see, as if inspired,
It was fate's way of educating us.
Remembering then when you were venomous,
You will be glad enough that I am gone,
But you will know more of what's going on;

For you will see more of what makes it go,
And in more ways than are for you to know.
We are so different when we are dead,
That you, alive, may weep for what you said;
And I, the ghost of one you could not save,
May find you planting lentils on my grave.

HECTOR KANE

If Hector Kane at eighty-five
Was not the youngest man alive,
Appearance had anointed him
    With undiminished youth.
To look at him was to believe
That as we ask we may receive,
Annoyed by no such evil whim
    As death, or time, or truth.

Which is to doubt, if any of you,
Seeing him, had believed him true.
He was too young to be so old,
    Too old to be so fair.
Beneath a snowy crown of curls,
His cheeks that might have been a girl's
Were certainly, if truth were told,
    Too rose-like to be there.

But Hector was a child of earth,
And would have held of little worth
Reflection or misgiving cast
    On his reality.

It was a melancholy crime,
No less, to torture life with time;
And whoso did was first and last
    Creation's enemy.

He told us, one convivial night,
When younger men were not so bright
Or brisk as he, how he had spared
    His heart a world of pain,
Merely by seeing always clear
What most it was he wanted here,
And having it when most he cared,
    And having it again.

"You children of threescore or so,"
He said, "had best begin to know
If your infirmities that ache,
    Your lethargies and fears,
And doubts, are mostly more or less
Like things a drunkard in distress
May count with horror, while you shake
    For counting days and years.

"Nothing was ever true for me
Until I found it so," said he;
"So time for me has always been
    Four letters of a word.
Time? Is it anything to eat?
Or maybe it has legs and feet,
To go so as to be unseen;
    Or maybe it's a bird.

"Years? I have never seen such things.
Why let your fancy give them wings
To lift you from experience
    And carry you astray?
If only you will not be old,
Your mines will give you more than gold,
And for a cheerful diligence
    Will keep the worm away.

"We die of what we eat and drink,
But more we die of what we think;
For which you see me still as young
    At heart as heretofore.
So here's to what's awaiting us—
Cras ingens iterabimus—"
A clutch of wonder gripped his tongue,
    And Hector said no more.

Serene and inarticulate
He lay, for us to contemplate.
The mortal trick, we all agreed,
    Was never better turned:
Bequeathing us to time and care,
He told us yet that we were there
To make as much as we could read
    Of all that he had learned.

THE MARCH OF THE
CAMERON MEN

An autumn twilight on a quiet lake;
A silent house, with more than silence in it;
A boat, and a man resting on his oars;
A woman with him, looking at the shore,
And inland where the house was, and the trees.

Since that was all there was to be a picture
That she was tired of seeing so long, she said:
"Row me into the middle of the lake,
Where there shall be no eyes, or possible ears,
To watch or listen. We are alone, you say;
But we are not alone who are so near
A shore alive with silence. I can hear it,
And feel it holding me. It has cold arms,
Like one of those unnecessary monsters
That God must once have hidden in the sea
Because he was afraid of his own work.
He has done much to make himself afraid,
And more to make us wonder why he does it.
No, I am not afraid. I am only saying
We are too near that house where silence lives."

"A most unlovely fancy, nevertheless,
  For one so lovely as you are," he said,
  And smiled at her: "Well, it will not be noisy
  Out there where we are going."

                              "We are going
So far," she said, "that we may not come back;
  Or not as we are now."

                              "I'll pray for that
While I am rowing; and you may as well
Pray also. There will be no harm in it,
And I shall see you—which is always prayer
For me, and prayer enough. . . . So here we
    are,
With not an ear to listen, or an eye
To watch. My eyes are occupied with you,
But yours are always looking at the water—
As if to see a monster with long arms.
You will not see him—not unless you find
His image in your fancy. By this time
You must have heard an inward little voice,
Saying that you are free."

                              "It is too soon,"
She said, "for me to hear too many voices,
Though I can hear a few that follow me.
And there are still our mortuary manners
To be remembered. We are not yet so free
That custom has forgotten us."

"Not yet;
And I deserve a ribbon and a cross
For not forgetting that. You know by now
A love as careful of its counterfeit
As it was careless of its cost. You know
By now, and with all said, how much there was
Not said—and all for manners. That was right,
And we shall hold ourselves a little closer
For not outreaching death. There was a lapse
That I regret. There was no more than one;
And there was one only because . . ."

"Be careful—
Or you will say it badly and be sorry.
And I can see no right that sorrow has
To follow us out here." She sought his eyes
With hers, and smiled as if to punish him.

"If I was careless once, it was because
Life made you as you are. How, I don't know.
No more have I a knowledge to define
A few not all celestial elements
That I would not see elsewhere than in you.
Although a doctor, I would not remove
Their presence, or transmute them. As you are,
You are more perilous than snakes and lions,
Or anything in the sea; and as you are,
You are more than a man's life; mine, or another's.
You drove me away once, but I came back.
I came because you said you needed me—

[73]

Because you called me. I could hear men march-
     ing,
And I was all those men. I was an army,
And you the banners that were over me.
In a forgotten tune that you were drumming
On dim keys, aimlessly, in a dark room,
I could hear drums and pipes down all the ages
That I had waited. I had come home again,
Where no home was for me. I could not stay,
And could not go; for there was a man dying,
Unless my skill should save him. It was you
Who called me back again; and we were there,
Together where darkness was. If you had
     willed it,
You might have driven me into this lake to
     drown—
Or possibly not quite. We'll say, perhaps,
You might have driven as much of me to die
As would have been worth living, and left the rest
To go on as it might, ingloriously.
Sparing me that, you drove me back to life.
You might have driven me then to anything.
You drove me once to song."

                              Waiting, he smiled,
And watched her fingers touching the cold lake
As if it scalded them. "If I did that,"
She said, "there must be power unfound in me,
Deserving a discovery. I dare say
If only more physicians would bring songs,

And sing them to us, they would save more lives.
What song is this of yours that I inspired?
Sing it, or say it. Was I playing it?"

"You played for me unseen; and as you played,
Music made words. I have not written them,
Or said them until now. Their only worth
Is in whatever there is of you in them—
Which, if assayed and analysed, appears
A little playful and equivocal:

> *'Any tune in the world would have told him*
>   *as well*
>   *As another of all that was there,*
> *For a beggar with only a story to tell*
>   *And a woman with nothing to spare.*
> *But you called, and a king who believed he*
>   *was dead*
>   *Was alive and undying again:*
> *It was you, and the night, and the stars over-*
>   *head,*
>   *And the March of the Cameron Men.'* "

"Yes, I remember—now," she said. "I played it
There in the dark. I don't know where it came
    from.
Where do things come from that are so forgotten
That we have lost them and the names of them,
And are not sure we had them? You were com-
    ing,

[75]

And I was calling you with an old tune
That must for years have hidden in my fingers,
Waiting for you to come. Were the stars hidden
From you until you heard it? I hope not."

He gazed at her uncertainly, and answered
As a man willing still to be assured:
"There was more hidden from me than the stars,
And you know that. All that I'm seeing now,
All that I waited for, and has been waiting,
Was hidden; and I was hidden from myself.
God, what it is for me to see you here—
You here, alone! I said there was an army
Marching along with me to find you there
That night, and so there was. It was an army
Of new days to be born of joy and hope,
A phantom regiment of realities
That now are—almost real. I hesitated
For the same reason that bewilders me
In seeing you here and saying it is you.
It may be well for us that we know slowly
What sorrow teaches; we know better then
What peace and freedom are when they are ours.
And freedom now is not for us alone;
For there's another free, there in that house—
The same house where I came and found you
        waiting.
You had been angry and implacable
So long before, and for so long been silent,
That I was nothing till I was a king:

'In your smile was a gift of ineffable things,
    And of more than all scholars have
      learned.
In a palace where beggars were richer than
      kings
    There was more to be given than earned.
Not a murmur remained of a storm that was
      past,
    Or of why it had happened, or when.
You had called, and he came; and he found
      you at last
    In the March of the Cameron Men.'

"You are still giving, and more than I shall earn
If I live always. Love has a way sometimes
Of giving and of hiding what it gives
Until it withers and is not the same—
Yet this is not an hour for telling you
So much less than you know. It seized me then,
Much as another stanza that I made
Came out of nowhere—and, as one too many
Has always done, troubled the other two
Until it recognized itself and vanished,
Leaving the two sufficient. Now you know
The sort of minstrel I might be, if urged,
And honor me the more as a physician.
You may as well rejoice within you also,
For your sake and for my sake, and for his,
For what has come to be . . . God, is it you—
At last! A smile would make me sure of you.

[77]

I am not asking you to laugh, you see—
Not now. Are you afraid I do not know?
Are you afraid that I'll forget myself
And be a fool—with him there, in that house?
No, I shall not do that."

                        "I'm not afraid,"
She said, and smiled for him. "But I am hearing
The marching feet of all those Cameron Men.
They are going, I suppose, to kill somebody,
Or to be killed themselves. I wonder why
So many of our songs and melodies
That help us to forget, and make us happy,
Are born of pain, and oftener of defeat
Than victory. I believe those lines of yours
Told all you knew, all you will ever know,
About the melancholy why of things—
Out of which hope was born."

                     "They were not made,"
He said, "to make you melancholy. Rather
I fancied you might recognize in them
A triumph coming to you from a distance,
Through a long darkness, to an open door
In your unhappy house. If you had been
Away from there, there would have been no house
Worth coming to; and if you had not smiled,
I should have gone again. Did you hear nothing
In those poor lines of mine to tell you so,
And make you happier for not sending me

[78]

Away from a closed door? Nature has done,
Since then, only as much as you have prayed for
With all but words. There was no need of words
To speak a wish or make a purpose clear
While you had eyes to ask. Did you get nothing
Of joy, or of release, or of thanksgiving
Out of those lines of mine?"

                "Surely I did,"
She said, "But you said only some of them.
I shall be surer when I have them all
Of what it is they say, and of what music
It was that I was making when you came.
Men marching all go somewhere—some to free-
    dom,
Some to captivity, and some to death.
The dead are free, I hope. I wish we knew.
Or—no, perhaps, I don't. Tell me the rest
Of that so joyful song you made for me
About those marching men. You should have said
It ended there, or should have given me all
There was of it to hear. Never since God
Made the first heart and ears that felt and waited,
Was anything not revealed less perilous
For leaving it half said."

               He studied her
And tried to laugh, but his accomplishment
Was only a small broken sound of doubt.
"Was it a woman who was saying that?"

[79]

He asked; and with a shrug that was a sort
Of answer to himself, he hesitated.
"There was an end of it that went like this,"
He said, "but it was meaningless to me,
As it will be to you. When a thing's done,
Only a novice goes on doing it:

> 'When he left you again there were stars in
>   the way
> Of his eyes, and he wandered alone
> In a dream that would mock him for many
>   a day
> With a music unheard and unknown;
> Till at last he awoke, and remembered, and
>   found
> All there was that remained of it then.
> There was only the sound of the world going
>   round,
> And the March of the Cameron Men.'

"Nothing, you see, to scare you or disturb you.
Nothing—or no more than a footed fancy
Chasing its tail. I would have let it go
And lost it as a vagrant—willing enough
To see no more of it. But I'll obey
My lady's humor when she bids me serve,
Although her whim may whistle me to danger.
There is no danger now. Why do you gaze
At everything but me? Why do you look
So long across the lake to see that house?

You cannot see it. There are too many trees.
And even if you should find it, and be in it,
You would be there alone. He is not there.
There's only an old garment all worn out—
A body that he was glad to leave behind.
What is he now but one far more a theme
For our congratulation than our sorrow?
There was no happiness in him alive,
And none for you in your enduring him
With lies and kindness. It was a wrong knot
You made, you two; and one knot more or fewer,
In a world where there are still so many knots,
Will be forgotten and will not be found
In the large histories. Why are you looking
At that place, always? Men will come tomorrow
And carry him away to his last home,
And to his first. There was no home on earth
For him, and none for you while he was here.
What is it makes you seek so curiously
For what you would not see if it were there?"

"Nothing. I thought I heard those Cameron Men.
Are they to march as long as I'm alive—
And over my grave, perhaps? . . . Yes, I re-
    member.
You asked a question that has had no answer.
Nothing—except that once I married him,"
She said, and waited with inquiring eyes.
She touched again the cold lake with her fingers,
And shivered as if she were there alone.

[81]

"A woman's fancy would go back to that,"
Said he, "and make her say it as a duty.
Her way of never letting go a thing
That's gone would make of healing and escape
A pleasant incubus to bite her dreams.
I have known prisoners, free at last, not wholly
At ease with freedom, or at home with it."

"What had your lawless friends been at," she asked,
"To be so loth to walk abroad again?
Had they been killing men? Had they been do-
      ing,
Not quite with our precaution and finesse,
What you and I have done so delicately?
Why start? We are free now, and are alone
On a cold lake; and a lake has no ears."

She pierced him with a look that blinded him
Until he saw that she was humorous,
Whereat he smiled at her uncomfortably,
And partly laughed at her. "My faults," he said,
"Are numerous and acknowledged, and are mine
For penance or for pardon, as may be.
I have seen opportunity like water
 Flow through my fingers when I might have
      held it;
I have been told the word I should have said,
And have been silent when I might have said it;
With a short road before me, I have followed
Trails that have ended only in the long

[82]

Forlorn way of return; with my eyes open,
I have walked into brambles and been scratched.
I am not blameless; I am not unsinged,
Or spotless, or unbitten. Have I said so?
Yet there is more of me than my mistakes,
Or you and I would hardly be together
Here in the middle of this chilly lake,
With night soon covering us. There's more of me,
Be sure, than a man asking for a woman
Who would not have him if she doubted him.
I'm farther from the pliocene than that;
And you would soon see in my care for you
How much of care there is in a man's love
When it is love—which is a little more
Than any myopic science isolates
With so much carnal pride. Now you are smil-
    ing—
Either because you doubt me, or believe
My doubts are talking. There is more of me,
I hope, than a pathetic mechanism
Grinding itself to nothing. Possibly not,
But let me say there is; and let me feel
Inside me that I've done more good than narm,
With my mistakes and opportunities
All marked against me on the other side.
Leaving an inventory to your fancy,
I'll only say that I see many alive
Who might be dead if I had never lived.
Some I have saved who might have loved me more
If I had let them go as they were going.

Sometimes I have imagined I was God,
And hesitated. I have seen the end,
Before their trial, of last and desperate
Experiments, and I have not suborned
The best of me in hastening nature's worst
Indignities of anguish and despair
To nature's end. I have done this before;
And if again—I shall have killed no man."

Once more she touched the water with her fin-
        gers,
And in the twilight smiled admiringly.
"A man's precision in extremities
Would say all that," she said, "and would forget
How it might sound if on a judgment day
Some God, or some inflexible magistrate,
Without your genius in the differences,
Might hear it and then make you say it over.
Your chivalry says 'I'—and mine says 'we'.
We have not killed him. We have let him die.
And we shall find him as we left him there.
He will not hear the sound of our return,
But we shall hear those Cameron Men, I think,
Still marching, always marching. I can hear them
Where we are now. You may have summoned
        them
With those last lines of yours—that meant so little
To you that you would rather not have said them
Aloud to me. Why do you think you made them?
Or, if they made themselves, what right had they

To make a music that in you already
Was marching when I called for you to come?"

A laughter for a moment in her eyes
Was like a flash of cruel triumph passing,
At which he scowled and wondered, and then
    smiled—
As the betrayed and the defeated smile.
"You have not scored so unapproachably
As to be laurelled or to live in song—
Or not for that," he said. "Am I the first
Who has confessed unwittingly misgivings,
Or premonitions, or the still small voice
That a man hears when he stakes everything
On Fate—whose name is yours? In face of all
The fairness of your magnanimity,
I'll still say that I did it. You are free.
I did it more for you than for my love—
Or so I did believe . . . God—is it you
That I am looking at! Are we alone—
Here on this lake together, and at last
With all that was intolerable behind us?
You are not thinking. You are only free,
And are not yet aware of what it means."

"Yes, I am free—if women are ever free;
And I am thinking—if a woman thinks.
You men, who from your scalps down to your toes
Are built of thought, are still debating it.
But I'll commit myself to your misgivings,

[85]

Your premonitions, and your still small voice,
And tell you what I think. . . . Horrors—hear
　　that!

The unearthly ululation of a loon
Tore the slow twilight like a mortal yell
Of madness, till again there was a silence.
"Fate punctuates our words and purposes,
　You see, and that was a full stop," he said:
"It may have been a way of warning you
To say no more—except that you are happy,
Or that you will be when all this is over.
Tomorrow they will carry him away,
Out of that house, to sleep and to be done
With all his persecutions. You are free
Of them all now. And you are free to think—
Of what you will."

　　　　　　　"I'll tell you what I think,"
She said; and her calm eyes were like a child's,
Waiting for the reward of his approval:
"I think that when a woman and a man
Are on their way to make of their two lives
Deliberate and ceremonial havoc,
There's folly in going on if one of them
Sees what's ahead, knowing the other sees it
And shuts his eyes. I have paid once for ruin,
And once will do. I thought, before I thought,
Before I knew, that I could see fair weather
For you and me, and only friendliness

[86]

In every natural sign that led me on—
Till I found nature waiting like a fox
For an unguarded pheasant. But I saw it
In time to fly away and save myself,
And, for my flying wisely, to save you.
There are some promises of mine, I know,
And they are best forgotten. If remembered,
They would be treasured more if broken and
    lost,
Like placeless remnants that are in most houses,
And in most lives. We stare at the old things,
Until they are all blurred with memories
That move and hum for us monotonously,
Like old ghosts playing on forgotten strings
We cannot see or hear. Your sound of the world
Going round is not unlike it."

                    A new chill
Now falling on the lake was not so cold
Or certain as a freezing realization
That gripped his heart. What sort of ignominy
Was this that pierced him with an innocence
More venomous than contempt? It was not that,
But might as well be as be what it was.
"You thought, before you thought," he said at last;
"And when you sent for me, was it before
You thought, or was it after? You should know,
And I should know. Nothing in life appears
To me of more importance than my knowing
Just when it was you called me, and for what.

[87]

I saw you, on my journey, in my arms
At a long journey's end, and saw you smiling;
And so you were—and you were in my arms.
Why was all that? Why should I let him die,
But for a vision of lost years filled only
With you, and one of other years before me
That were not to be lost—with you in them.
Was it all shadows, then, before and after,
And all the time? Was it a shadow playing
For me when I came back there in the starlight?
Was it a shadow that inveigled me
To serve as agent of a weariness
That owns no purpose and has no remorse?
I say remorse, for nothing is that's ours,
Not even the gift of love like mine for you,
That has the refuge of too sure a credit
Against the price of time. We gambled there,
And are we both to lose? By God, my lady,
If I have heard you and have learned your lan-
    guage,
A quieter place for you than in his house
Would be a place with him where he has gone.
You should have silent earth, or say the bottom
Of this benevolent lake, where all is quiet.
You will not like that house when he's not there,
More than when he was in it."

                              "No," she said,
And shivered. "I have had enough of it.
I have been there too long. He was a devil,

[88]

And should have gone before. God was afraid
To let him live. You would have been afraid,
If you had made him. As for you and me,
You would have nothing, if you drowned me now,
But sorrow for your work. I should have peace,
But you would only have those marching men
To follow until you tired of them and died.
Would you have that, and would you call it wis-
      dom?
Is it not better to be wise tonight,
And free tomorrow? To be wise and free
Has always been a dream for most of us,
And will remain a dream. Yet for a few—
For you and me—it will be real and easy,
If we will be ourselves. For your heart knows
More than it lets you say—as mine did once,
Before it let me think. His going away
Has left a clearness where it was all fog
While he was here. We shall see better now,
And there will be a time for you to bless me
That all has ended well. Some time or other
We shall see backward to this quiet hour,
Praising our wits because it was so quiet.
There is that loon again!—reminding us,
He says, that we have had his lake too long."

He sat with his head heavy in his hands,
Gazing at shadows. There was cold within him
Where triumph once alive had no life now.
There was not even anger to arouse it

Into false life again. "God—is it you?"
He said, and was not asking anything:
"And has it come to this? Is this the end?"

"Many have died for less than this, my friend,"
She answered; and her smile was like a blow
Dealt softly on his heart and staying there,
For time to cool and heal. "Now row me back,"
She said: "We must not be here in the dark.
He will be waiting for us, and will do us
No manner of harm. He will be there tonight,
But not tomorrow. We shall all go tomorrow.
I shall remember you, and pray for you;
And I shall always hear the Cameron Men."